SPRING HARVEST

I0801625

big start

annual 2

packed with fun-filled activities

CANDLE BOOKS

Welcome to Big Start Annual 2

How many hidden alarm clocks can you find in this annual?

You can find the Big Start theme song here:

You'll find this annual packed with stories, activities, games, jokes, family–time ideas, prayer and commitment prompts, and more all based on the theme "Up and Alive!"

The letter to the Ephesians in the New Testament of the Bible helps us to REMEMBER who God is and what Jesus has done for us. We need to be READY to live well with God's strength through the Holy Spirit and RISE up to lead the amazing life God wants for us.

A BIG thank you goes to all the contributors who have shared their work. So, pick up your pens and pencils and get ready to release your masterpiece!

Look out for the running lion!

Contents

Each section uses these symbols: Key

Story — Think — Reflect — Question — Think Pair Share

1. LOOK UP and remember who God is

God placed all things under his (Jesus') feet and appointed him to be head over everything for the church. (Ephesians 1:22)

Walking on Water

Jesus sent his disciples ahead of him, back across the lake. As night fell, Jesus climbed the hill overlooking the lake, to be alone with God his Father.

Meanwhile, the disciples were struggling desperately against a strong wind. However hard they rowed, they made no headway.

From the top of the hill Jesus could see the little boat and picture his exhausted disciples. He would go to them.

But when the disciples saw a mysterious shadowy figure coming towards them across the lake in the moonlight, they were terrified.

"It's a ghost!" they shrieked. Their tired nerves could stand no more.

Then a familiar voice rang out.

"Don't be frightened! I'm coming to help you!"

They could not believe it.

"If it's really you," Peter called back, "tell me to come to you."

"All right, Peter," Jesus answered, "come on!"

Peter climbed over the side of the boat and began to walk towards Jesus on top of the water. Suddenly he felt a strong gust of wind catch him and he looked down at the swirling waves. In that moment of panic he began to sink.

"Help! Save me, Lord!" he shouted. Jesus put out his hand quickly, caught Peter by the wrist and pulled him up from the foaming water.

"Why did you doubt me, Peter?" he asked.

Then the two of them climbed into the boat. Immediately the wind died down. The disciples were amazed. They could not understand how their master was able to do the impossible.

This story is taken from ***The Children's Bible in 365 Stories***.
9781915748010 (hbk) 9781915748027 (pbk),
written by Mary Batchelor and illustrated by John Haysom

Jesus wants to reach his friends' boat.
He is walking on the water
Which way will bring him to their boat?

The answer is on p.46.

Question

At first, the disciples were afraid they had seen a ghost.

What did Jesus say to the frightened disciples?

This story is found in the Bible: The Gospel of Mark, chapter 6, verses 45 to 51.

Jesus' friends were caught in a storm at sea. Jesus walked across the water to help them.

There are five funny mistakes in the picture. Can you find them all? Circle them. If you wish, colour the picture.

The answers are on p.46.

In this picture, the disciples look very surprised. Why do you think they look so surprised?

Colour the picture.

Did you know? Jesus came from heaven to earth to be with us and connect us with him. All things are under his feet. He has authority over all creation. Think about how this story about Jesus walking on water shows he has this authority.

LIGHTS! CAMERA! ACTION!

In films, directors sometimes use slow motion to make a scene really tense.

If a director was making a film about the story of Jesus walking on water, do you think they would use slow motion to make the storm scene dramatic?

Let's get creative!

A fun way of creating your own slow-motion scene from the story is to create a stop-motion video. By adding a series of photographs together, it can look like a moving picture but in slow motion.

STEP 1 Using items in your house (such as a washing-up bowl filled with water, a tub for a boat, and any small figures you may have), create a small set that you can move and photograph to tell the story.

STEP 2 Create a "shot list" for your story. This is where you write a list of all the photographs you want to take to make sure you capture the whole story. For stop motion to work really well, the smaller the changes between each photo, the better!

STEP 3 Set up your first "shot". In the correct order, slightly moving the objects for each picture, begin to take your photos.

STEP 4 Once you have taken your photos, you can either edit them together to make a stop-motion film or you can flick quickly through your photos to see the effect of the pictures moving!

TOP TIPS:

- Keep your camera on something like a pile of books to stop it from moving in between shots.
- Make very small changes to the set and figures between shots. When you add all the photos together, it gives a brilliant slow-motion effect!

These creative ideas are taken from ***Wow! Jesus*** ISBN 9781781284254, written by Martha Shrimpton and illustrated by Sarah Nolloth. Also available in this series is ***Wow! Christmas*** ISBN 9781781284247

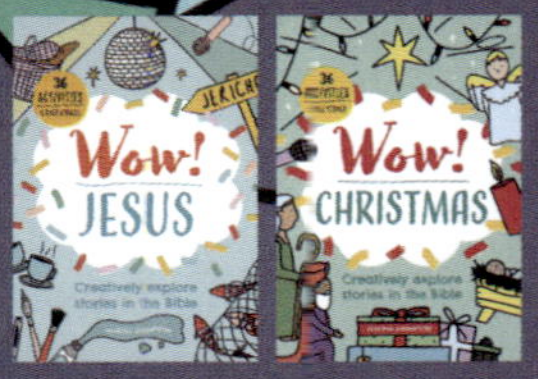

Wow! That's cool!

SWOOSH, WOOSH, TWIST, AND TURN

The disciples were so astounded by what Jesus did that they were even a little bit scared. His power was so great that he could walk on the water!

How do you think you would have felt if you had been there? Do you think you would have been amazed at Jesus' miracle? Sometimes, when we are overwhelmed with admiration for God, we can't help but worship him and praise him for his great power.

A great way to praise God is by using our bodies to worship him!

Let's get creative!

In this space, draw the shapes of the waves, twisting, turning, and crashing against the boat. Use shapes that are powerful and have curves as well as straight edges.

Look at the shapes you have drawn. With your whole body, recreate the shapes of the waves in large, powerful movements.

Play a piece of music and use the wave movements as worship to God for how powerful he is.

WALKING ON WATER

Jesus and Peter walk on the lake MARK 6

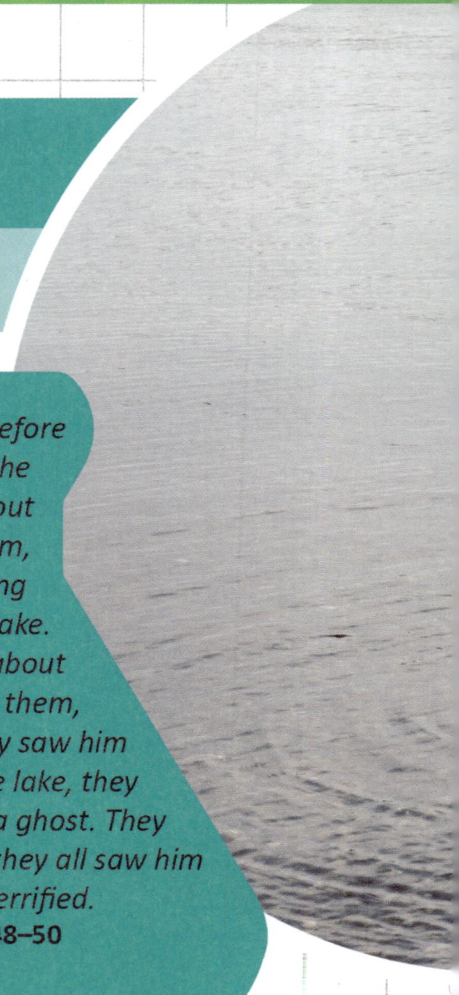

ON THE WATER

You need: glass, water, metal drawing pin (not plastic), washing up liquid

Clean the glass and the drawing pin with water and dry them. Fill the glass with water. Carefully place the pin on the water with the pin uppermost. Does the pin float? The washing up liquid is just like Peter's doubts. Add a small drop of washing up liquid to the water. What happens to the pin?

Shortly before dawn he went out to them, walking on the lake. He was about to pass by them, but when they saw him walking on the lake, they thought he was a ghost. They cried out, because they all saw him and were terrified.

Mark 6: 48–50

Immediately he spoke to them and said, 'Take courage! It is I. Don't be afraid.' Then he climbed into the boat with them, and the wind died down. They were completely amazed.

Mark 6: 50–51

What's happening?

The smallest particles in water are called water molecules. Water molecules attract one another and form a strong layer on the water surface. This layer is also called surface tension. The drawing pin will float on this layer. The washing up liquid destroys the surface tension and the drawing pin can no longer float.

A further thought:

But when you ask, you must believe and not doubt, because the one who doubts is like a wave of the sea, blown and tossed by the wind.

James 1:6

MIRACLES

POND SKATERS

Underneath their legs and belly pond skaters have got lots of tiny hairs. Between these hairs and the water there is a bit of air. This air pushes the water away and the surface tension of the water carries the insect so it doesn't sink. When you look at a pond skater you can see round shadows around its legs. These are the shadows of the dips it makes on the water's surface.

Tip: Try to spot a pond skater on a pond, a ditch or small lake.

CREATE A POND SKATER

You need: 3 thin bits of metal wire, small pliers, bowl of water

Twist two bits of wire together as shown in the diagram and bend the end bits away from each other. These are the front and hind legs. Twist the third piece of wire around the middle and create two more legs. Make sure all the legs are spread out a bit. Place your pond skater on the water.

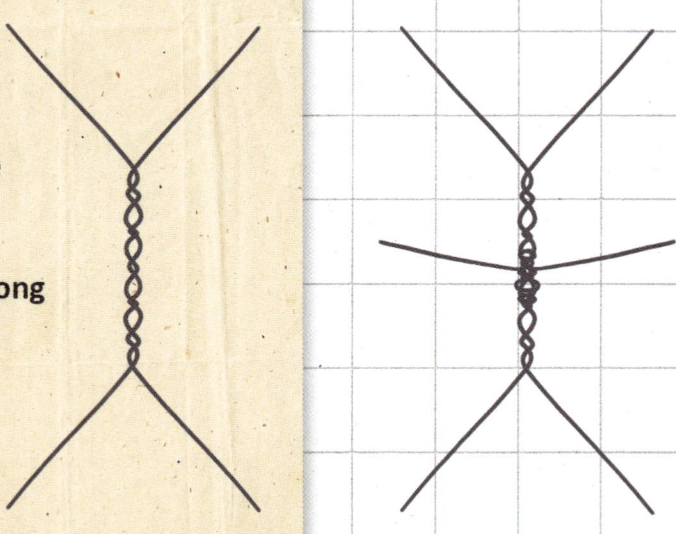

Tip: Instead of wire you can use three long bin bag fasteners, but you will need to remove the plastic layer first.

ASK AN ADULT TO HELP YOU.

These experiments are taken from ***Crackle and Pop: Bible Science Experiments*** ISBN 9780745978475, written by Hanna Holwerda and translated by Petra van Rijssen

God is bigger than everything and everyone. Let's praise him!

Look up!

Praise God, who made the world,
all the stars, and everything in space.

Look around!

Praise God, who made the plants,
all the animals, and every one of us.

These prayers are taken from ***Cheeky Pandas Prayer Paws*** ISBN 9781781284605 written and adapted by Paul Kerensa and Pete James, artwork from animations by Three Arrows Media think pair share

Think!

Can you remember this memory verse?

Use these actions.

God placed (point upwards)

all things (spread arms out wide)

under his feet (bend down low and put your hands under your feet)

and appointed him to be head (place an imaginary crown on your head)

over everything for the church (use open hands to draw a globe in front of you, from top to bottom)

Ephesians 1 (hold up one finger)

Verse 22 (use the other hand to flash 2 fingers, twice)

Pair and Share!

What words would you use to describe how big and amazing God is? Share your thoughts with your family and friends.

2. WAKE UP and remember who we are

For we are God's masterpiece. He has created us anew in Christ Jesus, so we can do the good things he planned for us long ago. (Ephesians 2:10)

The Little Girl

The boat with Jesus on board came in to land at a lakeside town. A great many people were gathered on the beach waiting to meet the famous teacher.

Jesus had hardly stepped ashore when a man named Jairus started pushing his way through the crowd. When the people saw who he was they made way for him, because he was a respected person in their community.

Although he was an important person, Jairus threw himself onto the ground at Jesus' feet. "Please help me, Teacher," he begged in tears. "My twelve-year-old daughter is dying. If you would only come to my house, I know that you could make her well!"

Jesus agreed to go with Jairus, but before they could reach the house, someone ran up to Jairus with a message. "Sir, your daughter has died," he said. "The Teacher cannot do anything to help you now."

Jairus was broken-hearted, but Jesus overheard the message. "Do not be afraid," he said calmly. "Trust me and believe, and she will be well."

When they arrived at the house, Jesus went inside with the child's parents and Peter, James and John.

The place was full of relatives who were crying because the little girl had died, but Jesus told them to be quiet. "Why are you making all this noise?" he asked. "The child is not dead – she is only sleeping!"

This only made the relatives angry: they jeered and argued, but Jesus took no notice of their complaints.

Instead, he entered the child's room with Jairus and his wife. Jesus went over to the bed where the girl was lying and took her hand in his. "Get up, my child!" he said. The girl's eyes flickered open and she sat up and smiled at her mother and father.

"Tell no one what has happened here," Jesus told the astonished parents. Then, looking across at the little girl, he added, "And give your daughter something to eat – she must be hungry."

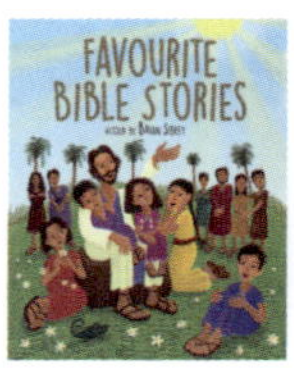

This story is taken from ***Favourite Bible Stories***, written by Brian Sibley and illustrated by Stephen Waterhouse ISBN 9780745979243. You can find more stories in ***The Empty Tomb: A Story of Easter*** ISBN 9780745979748

Join the dots to find out who is holding the girl's hand. Colour in the picture.

Question

Whct has happened to the little girl? What is her father's name?
This story is found in the Bible: The Gospel of Mark, chapter 5, verses 35 to 43.
(Answers on the next page.)

Jesus brings this little girl back to life.

There are four things in this picture which are mistakes – they didn't exist in Jesus' time. Cross out the mistakes.

The answers are on p. 46.

Did you know?

Jesus raised the little girl to a new and full life. We are also made fully alive in Christ as knowing Jesus changes us from the inside out. Think about how we might show Jesus' goodness to others.

Jesus healed the daughter of Jairus.

Find twelve (12) hidden doves in the picture.

The answers are on p. 46.

Jairus' daughter is alive again. The little girl's mother is preparing food for her to eat.

Complete the picture of Jairus' daughter after Jesus brought her back to life.

Look at the picture. How might the mother and daughter be feeling? What makes us fully alive?

Think!

Write this memory verse on a sticky note.

For we are God's masterpiece.
He has created us anew in Christ Jesus,
so we can do the good things he planned
for us long ago.

Ephesians, chapter 2, verse 10

Put the sticky note on a mirror to remind you that God made you for wonderful things.

Pair and share!

Try out this science experiment about transformation. How are our lives transformed from the inside out by knowing Jesus? Share your thoughts with your family and friends.

FROM ROCK-HARD TO SOFT

You need: raw egg, small bowl, vinegar

Carefully squeeze the egg. What does it feel like? Place the egg in the bowl. Immerse it in vinegar. Leave the egg to stand in the vinegar for 24 hours. Remove the egg from the bowl. Carefully squeeze the egg. What does it feel like now?

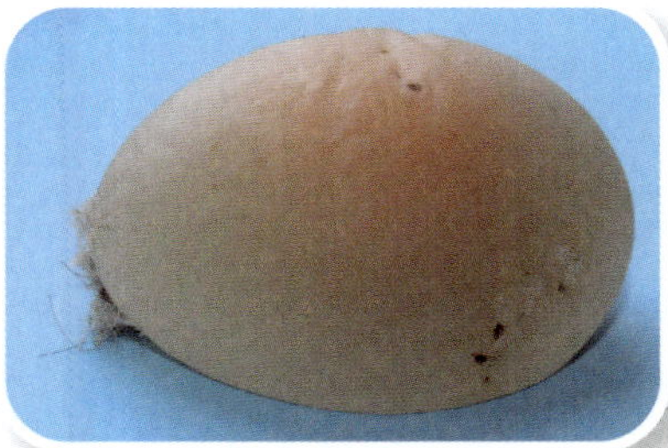

Soft-shelled eggs are eggs without the hard chalk shell. Young chickens sometimes lay this kind of egg.

What's happening?

The eggshell is made out of chalk. Chalk is hard. Underneath the shell there is a membrane (thin lining). Vinegar is acidic. Acid dissolves chalk. After 24 hours the eggshell has been dissolved and all that is left is the soft membrane containing the egg white and the yolk.

This experiment is taken from ***Crackle and Pop: Bible Science Experiments*** ISBN 9780745978475, written by Hanna Holwerda and translated by Petra van Rijssen

Q

What makes me me?

Dr Francis S. Collins,
Geneticist

Lots of things contribute to who you are. The DNA you inherit from your biological parents, the environment you grow up in, your experiences and opportunities all help to shape you in certain ways. But what really makes you you is the combination of all those things, plus your life choices. You become the unique person you are through the choices you make every day.

The Revd Dr Joanna Collicutt,
Neuropsychologist and Theologian

No two people are exactly the same – not even identical twins! Some important differences include our names, the things we like (food, music etc.), what we think is important, how we look, how we move, our funny little habits, where we call home, and the story of our lives. Above all I think what makes us who we are is who we love, and who loves us. For many of us, including me, God is a big part of that.

Prof. Tom Shakespeare FBA,
Sociologist, Broadcaster, Social Influencer

My genes, my upbringing, my education, my social background, gender, ethnicity, disability, and sexuality, the thousands of people I have met, the mistakes I have made, the chances I have taken and the experiences I have had, all combine to make me the unique and unrepeatable person I am. I believe we are made by God, wonderfully complex, and made up of so many different things.

Q

What does the Bible mean when it says we are "made in the image of God"?

Dr J. Richard Middleton, Theologian

The Bible says God made humans "in His image". But that doesn't mean we physically look like God. I think it describes the mission God has given us: to get to know Him in a special way and represent Him in the world. What does that look like? Well, although we can't literally see God, the Bible says He created the entire universe and loves everything He made - people, animals, plants, ecosystems, even stars and galaxies. So I think that when we love each other and look after this beautiful universe and the creatures that live here, we show God's love to the world. I believe we represent God by acting as He does.

It is also interesting that when the first part of the Bible was written, the phrase "image of god" was used to describe statues of gods and also powerful kings - not ordinary people. It meant that the statue or king was very special because they had the authority and responsibilities of a god. When the Bible says ALL people are made in God's image, I think it is saying how special God thinks all people are, and how much responsibility He gives us, to live and love like He does.

These questions and answers are taken from ***101 Great Big Questions About God and Science*** ISBN 9780745978369 coedited by Lizzie Henderson and Steph Bryant and illustrated by Andy Rowland

3. DRESS UP and remember what we need

Be strong in the Lord and in his mighty power. Put on the full armour of God. (Ephesians 6:10–11)

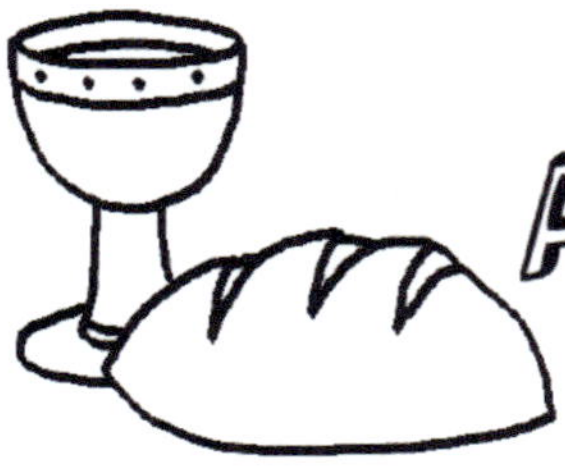

A NIGHT OF SURPRISES

Jesus was in Jerusalem. He was there to CELEBRATE the Passover feast, to REMEMBER how God had spared everyone whose house was marked with the blood of an innocent lamb.

He knew that he was about to die, just like that lamb. He even knew that his disciple, **JUDAS**, had agreed to BETRAY him to his enemies. So he arranged a place to eat. And he gathered with his disciples to share a meal. Then SURPRISE! he did something that no one else in the room expected. He took off his robe, tied a towel around his waist, filled a basin with water and began to wash his disciples' feet.

SIMON PETER spoke up, like he always did. 'Do you mean to wash my feet?' he asked. 'I do,' Jesus replied. 'And one day you will UNDERSTAND why'. 'No!' insisted Peter, shaking his head. 'You will never wash my feet!' Now perhaps Peter's feet were particularly **SMELLY** that day. More likely, he knew this was a servant's job and not

something that a MASTER, like a rabbi, should do. 'If I don't,' Jesus answered, 'you will not be a part of what I am doing.' 'Then wash me, head to toe!' Peter cried. When Jesus had washed their feet, **ALL** of their feet, even the feet of the man who had betrayed him, he put his robe back on. 'Do you **UNDERSTAND** what I have just done?' he asked. 'If I, your master, can wash your feet, then surely you can wash each other's feet. For a servant is not **GREATER** than his master. Know this. And more than that, do it. Serve one another!'

This story is taken from ***The Link-it-up Bible*** ISBN 9780281083022, written by Bob Hartman and illustrated by Gareth Williams

This excerpt from a story about helpfulness has been inspired by the Bible story of Jesus washing his disciples' feet and a real-life example from a grown-up.

A Great Day

We had out **new** kit on – **bright** purple and white, with **shining** black boots.

We played our best game EVER! I scored twice and the crowds cheered so loud

I thought my **big grin** would fall off my face!

When we **lifted** the trophy, Coach looked **so proud**.

He **wouldn t** say so, but I think he had a little tear in his eye.

After the game, we **celebrated** with hotdogs and milkshakes.

But when it was time for Coach to give a speech, he was **nowhere** to be seen.

I looked on the pitch – **not there**.
In the café – **not there**.
In the changing room, **not there** . . . or so I thought.

I could see all our muddy boots piled up and
Coach sitting behind them **lovingly**
cleaning them up ready for the next match.

What a guy! After **helping** us win, he **missed** the celebrations to do **ALL** the tidying up.

Coach is my **hero**. His **help** meant so much to our team.
Maybe I should be more like him and be a **good** team player in my family.

This excerpt is taken from one of the stories in ***Gemma Hunt's See! Let's Be A Good Friend*** ISBN 9780745979519, written by Gemma Hunt and illustrated by Charlotte Cooke

Also available in the series is ***Gemma Hunt's See! Let's Be Me*** ISBN 9780745998060 about exploring emotions and feelings with children

Question

**What is Jesus doing here?
What is he washing?**

This story is found in the Bible: The Gospel of John, chapter 13, verses 1 to 17.

Complete the picture.

think
pair
share

Think!

Jesus **took off** his outer garments and put on a towel to wash his disciples' feet. We need to be ready for whatever life might bring with God's strength and **take off** the things that hold us back. What might hold us back?

Read Ephesians chapter 4 to find out all kinds of things that we should **take off**.

This is a space to write or doodle your thoughts

Pair and share!

How are we equipped and ready for the life God calls us to live? Read Ephesians chapter 6 to find out some suggestions for what we can **put on**. Share your thoughts with your family and friends.

Can you remember this memory verse?

Imagine you are wearing the armour of God and use these actions.

Be strong in the Lord (hold up a big imaginary shield (of faith) in front of you)

and in his mighty power. (still holding the shield, use the other hand to hold out a big sword (of the Spirit))

Put on (touch your temples with both hands (helmet of salvation))

the full armour (cross your arms and touch both shoulders (breastplate of righteousness))

of God. (Put your hands on your waist (belt of truth))

(Then you can make a war-like shout of readiness as you bend over to touch your toes as fast as you can (feet ready to spread the gospel of peace))

Ephesians 6 (hold up six fingers)

Verses 10 to 11 (hold up 10 fingers and then 1 finger)

The armour of God may be invisible but with God's strength we can wear it every day.

Draw yourself wearing this armour into the blank box. Add a belt and hold a sword and a shield.

4. STAND UP and remember why we're here

Live as children of light…and find out what pleases the Lord. (Ephesians 5:8, 10)

You are a Child of God

Did you know? Have you heard the Good News?

While you are your mother and father's pride and joy,

you're also…wait for it…a child of God!

God has big plans for you!

He wants to help you grow to become completely the best self you can be…

the person He has made you to be.

To stay in His light to be holy, because you are a child of God!

However, if you should ever lose your way, and find yourself in a dark place.

Or if you might do something wrong, He'll help you make it right.

He will lead you back to the light.

For there's nothing you'd ever do to lose His love.

It's really true!

From morning until night, for the rest of your life and beyond,

God's love will always and forever surround you.

No matter what you say or do,

He'll always love and forgive you.

Because you – the wonderful, the glorious, the one-of-a-kind you –

you are His child.

You are a child of God.

This excerpt is taken from one of the chapters in ***God is Everywhere***
ISBN 9781781284155, written by Patricia J. Murphy and illustrated by Júlia Moscardó

Read the story in the Bible: The Gospel of John, chapter 8, verses 1 to 11.

Jesus went to the Mount of Olives. But early in the morning he went back to the Temple. All the people came to Jesus, and he sat and taught them. The teachers of the law and the Pharisees brought a woman there. She had been caught in adultery. They forced the woman to stand before the people. They said to Jesus, "Teacher, this woman was caught having physical relations with a man who is not her husband. The law of Moses commands that we kill with stones every woman who does this. What do you say we should do?" They were asking this to trick Jesus so that they could have some charge against him.

But Jesus **knelt down** and started writing on the ground with his finger. They continued to ask Jesus their question. So he **stood up** and said, "Is there anyone here who has never sinned? The person without sin can throw the first stone at this woman." Then Jesus **knelt down** again and wrote on the ground.

Those who heard Jesus began to leave one by one. The older men left first, and then the others. Jesus was left there alone with the woman. She was standing before him. Jesus **stood up** again and asked her, "Woman, all of those people have gone. Has no one judged you guilty?"

She answered, "No one has judged me, sir."

Then Jesus said, "So I also don't judge you. You may go now, but don't sin again."

Did you know?

Jesus stood up for the woman and then sent her away to stand up for him. We are encouraged to live Jesus' way and stand humbly and confidently. It takes courage and a strong faith in God to make this choice. We are not alone.

Wow! Can we chat?

SPEAKING WITH YOUR BODY

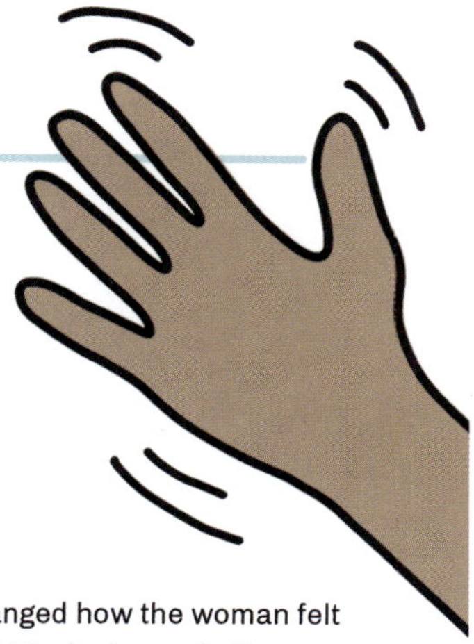

Quite often, when we feel something on the inside it will show in our body language on the outside. Different emotions and feelings can make us look different in the way we stand or walk.

Let's act!

Do you think the woman looked different after this experience with Jesus compared with how she looked before?

How do you think the woman felt at the start of the story? Can you use your body to show how the woman stood before the people?

Do you think Jesus changed how the woman felt at the end of the story? Maybe he made the woman feel loved and respected!

Can you use your body to show the change in the way the woman stood before Jesus?

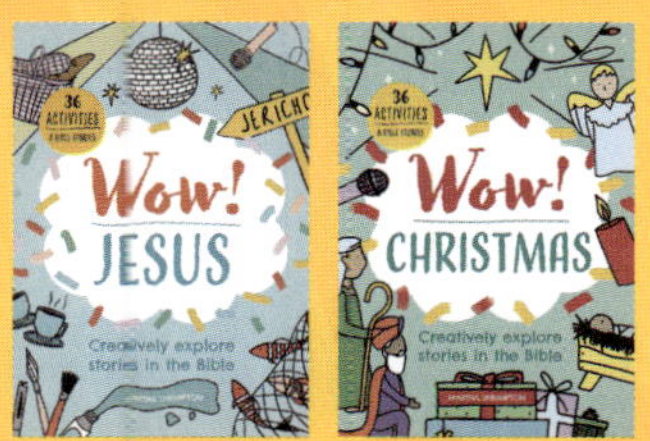

These creative ideas are taken from ***Wow! Jesus*** *ISBN* 9781781284254, written by Martha Shrimpton and Illustrated by Sarah Nolloth. Also available in this series is ***Wow! Christmas*** ISBN 9781781284247

When was the last time you had to be strong?

When was the last time you had to stand up and do the right thing, and not just the thing everyone else was doing?

What do you remember about how you felt when you stood strong?

Here is a prayer you can pray

O God,
give me the strength and heart and mind
to do the things that are good and kind.
O God,
may I face every task
with courage and cheerfulness.

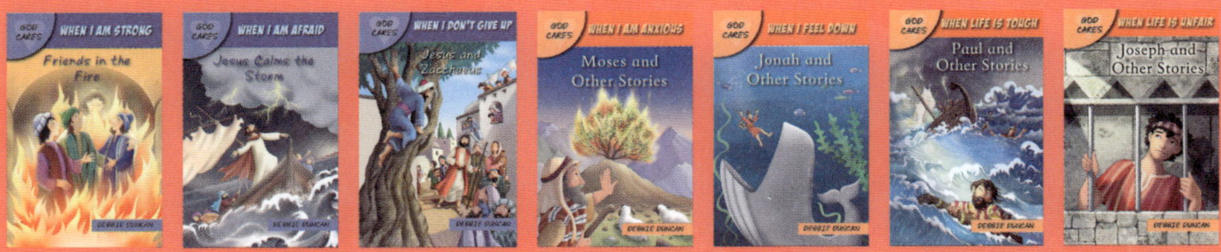

This reflection is taken from **God Cares: When I am Strong** ISBN 9781781283752, written by Debbie Duncan, which is part of the God Cares series – a biblical approach to children's wellbeing

This is a space to write or doodle your own prayers

think pair share

Think!

Write this memory verse on a sticky note and put it on a mirror to encourage you.

Live as children of light…and find out what pleases the Lord.
Ephesians, chapter 5, verses 8 and 10

Celebrate daily

Celebrate every day that you are a child of God! You can do this by praising God's name in prayer or in song, reading the Bible, and attending church regularly. These things will fill your heart and life with joy, and please God, too.

Activity

Use a plain t-shirt and fabric paints or pens to make a special "You are a child of God" t-shirt, or decorate plant pots using permanent markers with these words to give as gifts.

How can you bring light in different situations?

Pair and share!

Share your thoughts with your family and friends, and pray together. Ask God to help you to live as light and do the right things.

What could you do? Here are some ideas to get started:

- Be kind and helpful.
- Be loving towards others.
- Share your things with others.
- ______________________________
- ______________________________
- ______________________________

The activity is taken from ***God is Everywhere*** ISBN 9781781284155, written by Patricia J. Murphy and illustrated by Júlia Moscardó

Join team Joe for some sporty jokes and fun facts.

Did you know?

Three sports are mentioned in the Bible – wrestling, boxing, and running.

Frozen cow poo was the first-ever puck used in an ice hockey game.

OOOOOOOOOO!

Football (soccer) is the most popular sport in the world, with over 4 billion fans!

OOOOOOOOOO!

There are over 8,000 different sports played around the world but only 34 played at the Olympics.

The longest recorded tennis match lasted for 11 hours.

One sport has been played on the moon - golf.

Table tennis balls can travel off the bat at 105 miles per hour (mph), **golf balls** can reach speeds of 170 mph.

In Thailand, kite-flying is a professional sport.

OOOOOOOOOO!

Ha, ha, ha!

Why are fish rubbish at tennis?
Answer
They're scared of the net.

Don't tell a joke when you are ice skating.
Answer
The ice will crack up.

HA HA HA HA!

What android won the Olympic water sports?
Answer
The Rowbot

HA HA HA HA!

Adam should have got a gold medal!
Answer
He was first in the human race.

What is harder to catch, the faster you run?
Answer
Your breath

What tea do footballers drink?
Answer
Penal-tea

HA HA HA HA!

Why was the hairdresser disqualified from the race?
Answer
She took a short cut.

What is your favourite sporty joke and fun fact?
Write them here.

5. RISE UP and release your masterpiece!

I want you to get out there and walk – better yet, run! – on the road God called you to travel. (Ephesians 4:1)

Jesus is King!

Where's this in the Bible?

Acts 1

After God had raised him from the dead, Jesus stayed for 40 days with his disciples, teaching and encouraging them.

They knew from the Bible that God had promised to raise up a true king who would be Lord of all the earth, and who would bring justice and peace to his people.

"When will this happen?" asked the disciples.

Jesus explained that it would happen soon, but not in the way they were expecting. He said he would have to go away, and they would no longer be able to see him. But he would still be with them, helping and guiding them by God's Holy Spirit.

From now on, Jesus would be ruling the world from his new position at God's right hand. Jesus would be in heaven and God's new way of ruling the world would come true on earth.

"This is what will happen," said Jesus. "You will receive the power of God's Spirit. Then you will begin to tell the world all about me. You'll start in Jerusalem, then you'll go to Judea and Samaria, and then on and on to the ends of the earth!"

As Jesus said this, he was lifted up from them, and a cloud took him out of their sight.

Jesus' disciples were excited to know that he was now ruling the world in a whole new way, even though they couldn't see him. They prayed that he would begin to do the wonderful new things he had promised.

This story is taken from ***My Big Story Bible: 140 Faithful Stories, from Genesis to Revelation***
ISBN 9780281085613, written by Tom Wright and illustrated by Helena Perez Garcia

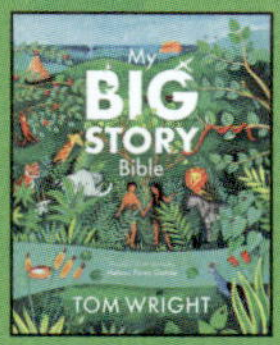

5 What goes in must come out

What's Up WOW

Apparently, if you eat a lot of beetroot you will have purply red poo and pink wee!

What goes in must come out!

It's basic science, right?

We see it everywhere . . .

If we drink loads and loads of water, eventually it'll have to **come out**, and we'll find ourselves with our legs crossed, shouting, "I need a wee, I need a weeeeeee!"

If we watch a scary movie, it might **come out** again in a bad dream.

If you eat a mega spicy curry, that has to **come out**, too. Probably into the loo . . . (Let's not go into too much detail there.)

Imagine squeezing an orange really hard with the skin on. Whatever is inside will come out . . . *hopefully just orange juice*!

If we fill our heads and hearts with God's truth – by reading the Bible and listening to worship songs – that's what will come out when WE are squeezed . . . even in the most challenging times.

Now that's the kind of **juice** I want coming out of me!

This is one of the devotions taken from ***What's Up*** ISBN 97819915749017
written by Joanna Adeyinka-Burford and designed and illustrated by Patrick Laurent

DEAR JESUS,

Help me to be wise about the things I put into my life. I know that the things I watch, read, and listen to have an effect on me. Help me to make good choices and put healthy things into my mind, body, and soul. In Jesus' name. Amen

Super smoothie

Design your perfect smoothie. Remember: put good things in and good things will come out!

What's Up challenge

What great things can you **put into** your life this week? Why not try learning a Bible verse? You never know - it might just **come out** when you or someone else needs it this week.

This week I am going to...

Did you know?

Jesus promised that his followers will be filled with the Holy Spirit, and this will help them to tell everyone about him all over the world! After Jesus had said this, he was raised up to heaven.

Read the story in the Bible: The Acts of the Apostles, chapter 1, verses 1 to 14.

Colour the picture.

Think about the ways that you could rise up and radiate God's Spirit in peace, love, and unity with others. Is there someone you could tell about Jesus today?

think
pair
share

Think!

Can you remember this verse?

Use these actions.

I want you to get out there and walk (march on the spot)

– better yet, run! (run on the spot)

– on the road God called you to travel. (swing with arms forwards and backwards as run and shout out the line)

Ephesians, chapter 4, (hold up four fingers on one hand)

Verse 1 (flash one finger with the other hand)

What do you think God is sending you out to do?

Although at times this may be hard, a holy life is adventurous and glorious.

Use this space to doodle or write your thoughts.

Pair and share!

Share your thoughts with your family and friends, and pray together. Here are the key points:

- Praise God that he is bigger than everything and everyone.
- Thank God for re-creating us anew in Christ Jesus and for all the good things he has planned for us.
- Thank God that we have everything we need to be strong and ready for whatever life might bring.
- Ask God to help us to stand up, filled with the Holy Spirit, and do what's right in Jesus' name.
- ____
- ____
- ____

Answers

Page 7

Page 8

Page 18

Page 19

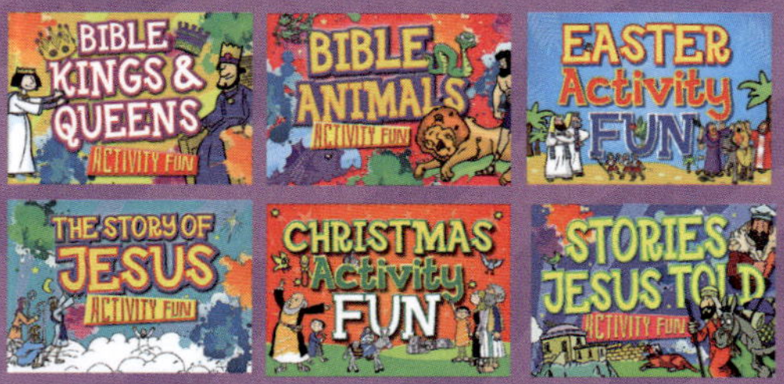

Activity sheets are taken from Candle Activity Fun series sold in packs ***The Story of Jesus*** ISBN 9781781284292 and ***Easter*** ISBN 9781781283721. Also available ***Christmas*** ISBN 9781781283837, ***Stories Jesus Told*** ISBN 9781781284285, ***Bible Kings and Queens*** ISBN 9781781284308, ***Bible Animals*** ISBN 9781781284094

There are 6 hidden alarm clocks in this book.